Introduction

The same three blocks are used in various combinations and an assortment of colors to make the table toppers in this book.

Paper-pieced triangle units eliminate the need to cut exact-size pieces and cut down the time needed for the construction process. All pieces can be rotary-cut to save time.

You won't be able to stop with just one table topper—by the time you complete one, you will be hooked and want to try them all.

Meet the Designer
Pat Campbell

Idaho designer/quilter Pat Campbell comes from two long lines of interesting and artistic ancestors. There were certainly quilters, but there were also people like the itinerant preacher who was a "dream reader" of note, a pioneer female doctor and her husband who made violins. Her father made jewelry and furniture, and he and Pat's mother built their house from design to finish. There were several generations of writers, poets and artists, including Pat's mother, who gained at least local fame.

Pat says all of these artistic abilities trickled down to her and her sister Nancy Nogues. Both are doodlers, fabric lookers and feelers, and quilt-pattern designers.

Pat spent two years studying commercial art at college before deciding that wasn't really what she wanted. She got a job, married and had two children, and somewhere in those busy years, she made her first quilt for the birth of her daughter. She says she still has the quilt, and "it's a pretty pathetic thing," but it did get her started making quilts.

At about the same time, she became interested in writing. After publishing a book of poetry in 1975 and two more in 1984, she took on the job of writing a short informational/humorous weekly column for the local newspaper.

In 1985, Pat found quilting again. This time it clicked, and she started her own home-based quilt-pattern business, Campbell Creations.

Pat's patterns sold quite well locally, and it gave her the confidence to submit some of her patterns to *Quilt World* magazine. She says it was the bravest thing she ever did.

In 1996 Pat published the book *Ships of the World: Foundation-Pieced Sailing Ships* which was sold all over the United States. She is currently working on several more quilt-book ideas, a book of cartoons and a book of Idaho Haiku.

Nine-Patch/ Roman Stripe Topper

Make a colorful topper using a Simple Nine-Patch block in a variety of color combinations with Roman Stripe blocks and units in a diagonal set.

PROJECT SPECIFICATIONS
Skill Level: Beginner
Quilt Size: 34" x 34"
Block Size: 6" x 6"
Number of Blocks: 24

MATERIALS
- ¼ yard each pink and gold mottleds
- ⅓ yard dark blue tonal
- ½ yard light blue tonal
- ⅝ yard light green tonal
- 1 yard dark green tonal
- Backing 40" x 40"
- Batting 40" x 40"
- All-purpose thread to match fabrics
- Quilting thread
- Basic sewing tools and supplies

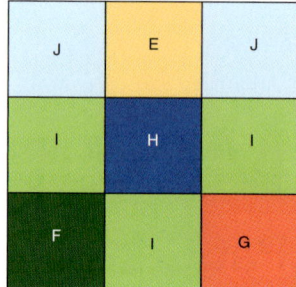

Corner Nine-Patch
6" x 6" Block
Make 4

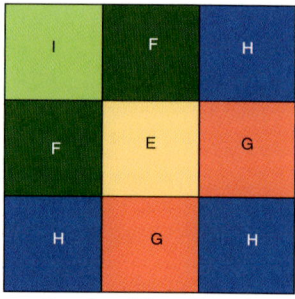

Center Nine-Patch
6" x 6" Block
Make 4

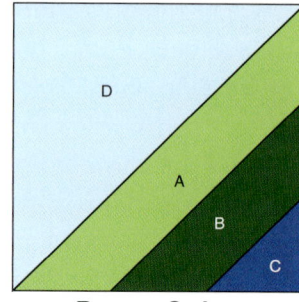

Roman Stripe
6" x 6" Block
Make 8

Side Nine-Patch
6" x 6" Block
Make 4

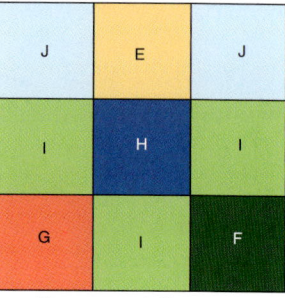

Reversed Corner Nine-Patch
6" x 6" Block
Make 4

Cutting

1. Make 24 copies of the Roman Stripe Paper-Piecing Pattern on page 31.

2. Cut six 2" by fabric width strips dark green tonal; subcut strips into (16) 10" A strips and eight 7" B strips.

3. Cut two 2½" by fabric width F strips dark green tonal; subcut one strip into two 10½" strips.

4. Cut four 2¼" by fabric width strips dark green tonal for binding.

5. Cut one 3¼" by fabric width strip each light and dark blue tonals; subcut strips into four 3¼" squares each fabric. Cut each square in half on one diagonal to make eight C triangles each fabric.

6. Cut two 2½" by fabric width H strips dark blue tonal; subcut one strip into three 10½" strips.

7. Cut one 6⅞" by fabric width strip light blue tonal; subcut strip into four 6⅞" squares. Cut each square in half on one diagonal to make eight D triangles.

8. Cut two 2½" by fabric width J strips light blue tonal; subcut one strip into two 10½" strips and one 21" strip.

9. Cut two 2½" by fabric width E strips gold mottled; subcut one strip into two 10½" strips.

10. Cut one 2½" by fabric width G strip pink mottled; subcut strip into one 21" and two 10½" strips.

11. Cut one 3¼" by fabric width strip pink mottled; subcut strip into four 3¼" squares. Cut each square in half on one diagonal to make eight C triangles.

12. Cut five 2" by fabric width strips light green tonal; subcut strips into eight 10" A strips and (16) 7" B strips.

13. Cut three 2½" by fabric width I strips light green tonal; subcut one strip into one each 10½" and 21" strip.

Completing the Roman Stripe Blocks

1. Complete eight dark blue and four each light blue and pink Roman Stripe triangle units using A and B strips and C triangles and referring to Figure 1 and the General Instructions on page 29.

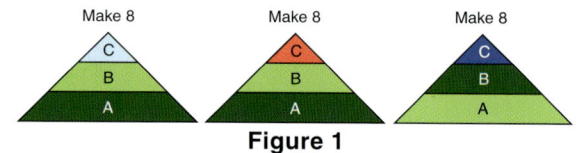

Figure 1

2. Add a D triangle to the A side of each dark blue unit to complete eight Roman Stripe blocks referring to the block drawing; press seams toward D.

3. Set aside the remaining triangle units for use when completing the top.

Completing the Nine-Patch Blocks

Note: Be careful when squaring one end of the strip sets to cut off only a very narrow section.

1. Join the 2½" x 10½" strips with right sides together along the length to complete strip sets as follows referring to Figure 2: I-F-H; F-E-G; H-G-H; and J-E-J. Press seams in directions indicated by arrows.

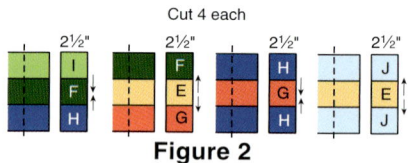

Figure 2

2. Subcut each strip set into four 2½" segments, again referring to Figure 2.

3. Join the 2½" by fabric width strips with right sides together along the length to complete one strip set each E-H-I and J-I-F as shown in Figure 3. Press seams in directions as indicated by arrows.

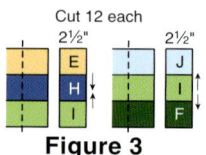

Figure 3

4. Subcut each strip set into (12) 2½" segments, again referring to Figure 3.

5. Join the 2½" x 21" strips with right sides together along the length to complete a J-I-G strip set as shown in Figure 4. Press seams in directions as indicated by arrows.

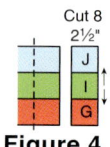

Figure 4

6. Subcut the strip set into eight 2½" segments, again referring to Figure 4.

7. Join one each I-F-H, F-E-G, and H-G-H segment to complete one Center Nine-Patch block referring to Figure 5; press seams in one direction. Repeat to make four blocks.

Figure 5

8. Join one each J-I-F, E-H-I and J-I-G segment to complete one Corner Nine-Patch block referring to Figure 6; press seams in one direction. Repeat to make four Corner Nine-Patch blocks.

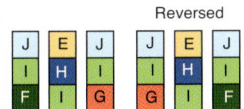

Figure 6

9. Repeat step 8, reversing color placement of segments to make four Reversed Corner Nine-Patch blocks, again referring to Figure 6.

10. Join one each J-I-F, E-H-I, and J-E-J segment to complete one Side Nine-Patch block referring to Figure 7; press seams in one direction. Repeat to make four Side Nine-Patch blocks.

Figure 7

Completing the Quilt

1. Arrange and join the completed blocks in diagonal rows with the light blue and pink triangle units as shown in Figure 8; press seams in adjacent rows in opposite directions.

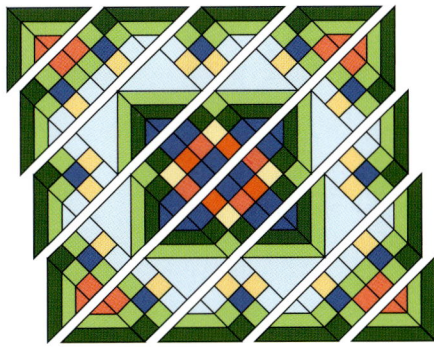

Figure 8

2. Join the rows to complete the pieced top; press seams in one direction.

3. Complete the quilt using the prepared backing and batting pieces and the cut binding strips referring to Completing Your Quilt on page 30.

Nine-Patch/Roman Stripe Topper
Placement Diagram
34" x 34"

Roman Stripe Festival

Two different blocks in a variety of colors create an exciting design.

PROJECT SPECIFICATIONS
Skill Level: Beginner
Quilt Size: 48" x 48"
Block Size: 6" x 6"
Number of Blocks: 64

MATERIALS
All fabrics are tonals, mottleds or solids
- ⅛ yard each light, medium and dark aqua and medium blue, medium red and medium green
- ¼ yard each pale aqua and light and dark blue
- ⅓ yard each dark red and darkest blue
- ½ yard each pink and darkest red and dark green
- ⅔ yard light green
- ¾ yard darkest green
- Backing 54" x 54"
- Batting 54" x 54"
- All-purpose thread to match fabrics
- Quilting thread
- Basic sewing tools and supplies

Cutting
1. Make 56 copies of the Roman Stripe Paper-Piecing Pattern on page 31.

2. Cut two 6⅞" x 6⅞" squares pale aqua; cut each square in half on one diagonal to make four D triangles.

3. Cut two 3¼" x 3¼" squares light aqua; cut each square in half on one diagonal to make four C triangles.

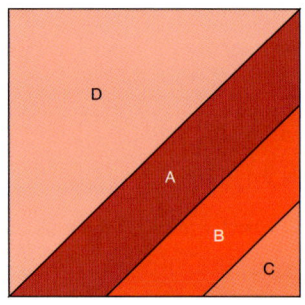

Red Roman Stripe
6" x 6" Block
Make 16

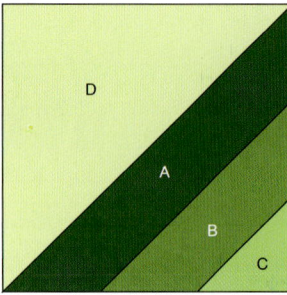

Green Roman Stripe
6" x 6" Block
Make 28

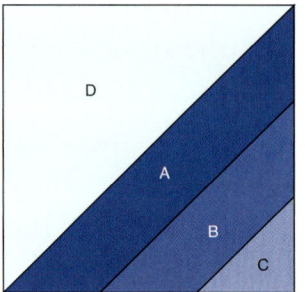

Blue Roman Stripe
6" x 6" Block
Make 8

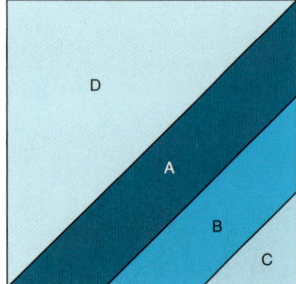

Aqua Roman Stripe
6" x 6" Block
Make 4

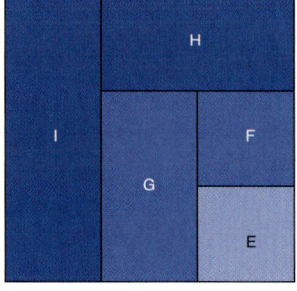

Blue Log Cabin
6" x 6" Block
Make 4

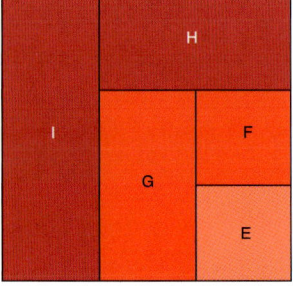

Red Log Cabin
6" x 6" Block
Make 4

4. Cut one 2" by fabric width strip each dark (A) and medium (B) aqua; subcut strips into four each 10" A and 7" B strips.

5. Cut four 6⅞" x 6⅞" squares light blue; cut each square in half on one diagonal to make eight D triangles.

6. Cut one 3¼" by fabric width strip medium blue; subcut strip into four 3¼" squares. Cut each square in half on one diagonal to make eight C triangles. Trim the remainder of the strip to 2½"; subcut strip into four 2½" E squares.

7. Cut two 2" by fabric width strips each darkest (A) and dark (B) blue; subcut strips into eight each 10" A and 7" B strips.

8. Cut two 2½" by fabric width strips darkest blue; subcut strips into four each 4½" H and 6½" I rectangles.

9. Cut one 2½" by fabric width strip dark blue; subcut strip into four each 2½" F squares and 4½" G rectangles.

10. Cut two 6⅞" by fabric width strips pink; subcut strips into eight 6⅞" squares. Cut each square in half on one diagonal to make 16 D triangles.

11. Cut one 3¼" by fabric width strip medium red; subcut strip into eight 3¼" squares. Cut each square in half on one diagonal to make 16 C triangles. Trim the remainder of the strip to 2½"; subcut strip into four 2½" E squares.

12. Cut three 2" by fabric width strips dark red; subcut strips into (16) 7" B strips.

13. Cut one 2½" by fabric width strip dark red; subcut strip into four each 2½" F squares and 4½" G rectangles.

14. Cut four 2" by fabric width strips darkest red; subcut strips into (16) 10" A strips.

15. Cut two 2½" by fabric width strips darkest red; subcut strips into four each 4½" H and 6½" I rectangles.

16. Cut three 6⅞" by fabric width strips light green; subcut strips into (14) 6⅞" squares. Cut each square in half on one diagonal to make 28 D triangles.

17. Cut two 3¼" by fabric width strips medium green; subcut strips into (14) 3¼" squares. Cut each square in half on one diagonal to make 28 C triangles.

18. Cut five 2" by fabric width strips dark green; subcut strips into (28) 7" B strips.

19. Cut seven 2" by fabric width strips darkest green; subcut strips into (28) 10" A strips.

20. Cut five 2¼" by fabric width strips darkest green for binding.

Completing the Roman Stripe Blocks

1. Complete four aqua, eight blue, 16 red and 28 green Roman Stripe paper-pieced triangle units using A and B strips and C triangles and referring to Figure 1 and the General Instructions on page 29.

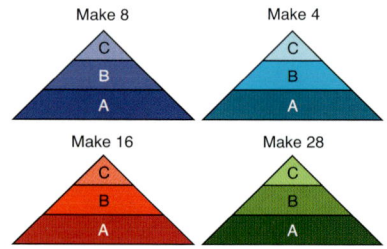

Figure 1

2. Add D triangles to the A side of each unit to complete the Roman Stripe blocks referring to the block drawings.

Completing the Log Cabin Blocks

1. Select E, F, G, H and I pieces from the blue color family.

Continued on page 32

Nine-Patch Crossroads

Two different Nine-Patch blocks and a Roman Stripe block combine to make this summery-looking topper or wall quilt.

PROJECT SPECIFICATIONS
Skill Level: Beginner
Quilt Size: 22" x 22"
Block Size: 6" x 6"
Number of Blocks: 9

MATERIALS
- 1 fat quarter red mottled
- 1 fat quarter yellow tonal
- ½ yard aqua mottled
- ⅝ yard white tonal
- Backing 28" x 28"
- Batting 28" x 28"
- All-purpose thread to match fabrics
- Quilting thread
- Basic sewing tools and supplies

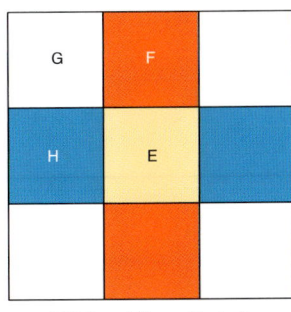

White Nine-Patch
6" x 6" Block
Make 4

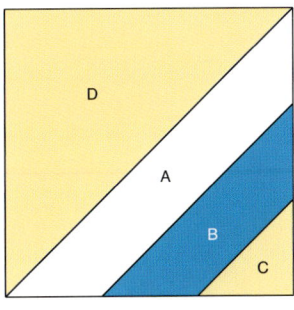

Roman Stripe
6" x 6" Block
Make 4

Blue Nine-Patch
6" x 6" Block
Make 1

Cutting

1. Make four copies of the Roman Stripe Triangle Paper-Piecing Pattern on page 31.

2. Cut one 2" by fabric width strip white tonal; subcut strip into four 10" A strips.

3. Cut one 2½" by fabric width strip white tonal; subcut the strip into two 21" G strips.

4. Cut two 2½" x 18½" I strips and two 2½" x 22½" J strips white tonal.

5. Cut one 2" by fabric width strip aqua mottled; subcut strip into four 7" B strips.

6. Cut two 2½" by fabric width strips aqua mottled; cut each strip in half to make four 21" H strips. Set aside one strip for another project.

7. Cut three 2¼" by fabric width strips aqua mottled for binding.

8. Cut two 3¼" x 3¼" squares yellow tonal. Cut each square in half on one diagonal to make four C triangles.

9. Cut two 6⅞" x 6⅞" squares yellow tonal; cut each square in half on one diagonal to make four D triangles.

10. Cut one 2½" x 21" E strip yellow tonal.

11. Cut three 2½" x 21" F strips red mottled.

Completing the Roman Stripe Blocks

1. Complete four Roman Stripe triangle units using A and B strips and C triangles and referring to the General Instructions on page 29.

2. Add a D triangle to the A side of each unit to complete six Roman Stripe blocks referring to the block drawing.

Completing the White Nine-Patch Blocks

1. Sew an H strip between two G strips with right sides together along the length to make a G-H strip set; press seams toward H.

2. Subcut the G-H strip set into eight 2½" G-H units as shown in Figure 1.

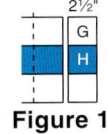

Figure 1

3. Sew an E strip between two F strips with right sides together along the length to make an E-F strip set; press seams toward F strips.

4. Subcut the E-F strip set into five 2½" E-F units as shown in Figure 2. Set aside one E-F unit for the Blue Nine-Patch block.

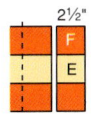 

Figure 2 **Figure 3**

5. Sew an E-F unit between two G-H units to complete one White Nine-Patch block as shown in Figure 3; press seams toward the E-F units. Repeat to make four White Nine-Patch blocks.

Completing the Blue Nine-Patch Block

1. Sew an F strip between two H strips with right sides together along the length to make an F-H strip set; press seams toward F.

2. Subcut the F-H strip set into two 2½" F-H units as shown in Figure 4.

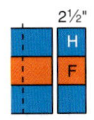 

Figure 4 **Figure 5**

3. Sew the F-H units to opposite sides of the previously set-aside E-F unit to complete one Blue Nine-Patch block referring to Figure 5; press seams toward the F-H units.

Completing the Quilt

1. Referring to the Placement Diagram, join two Roman Stripe blocks with one White Nine-Patch block to make the top row; repeat to make the bottom row. Press seams toward the Roman Stripe blocks.

2. Referring to the Placement Diagram, sew a Blue Nine-Patch block between two White Nine-Patch blocks to make the center row; press seams toward the Blue Nine-Patch block.

3. Sew the center row between the top and bottom rows to complete the pieced center; press seams in one direction.

4. Sew an I strip to opposite sides and J strips to the remaining sides of the pieced center; press seams toward the I and J strips to complete the pieced top.

5. Complete the quilt using the prepared backing and batting pieces and the cut binding strips referring to Completing Your Quilt on page 30. ∎

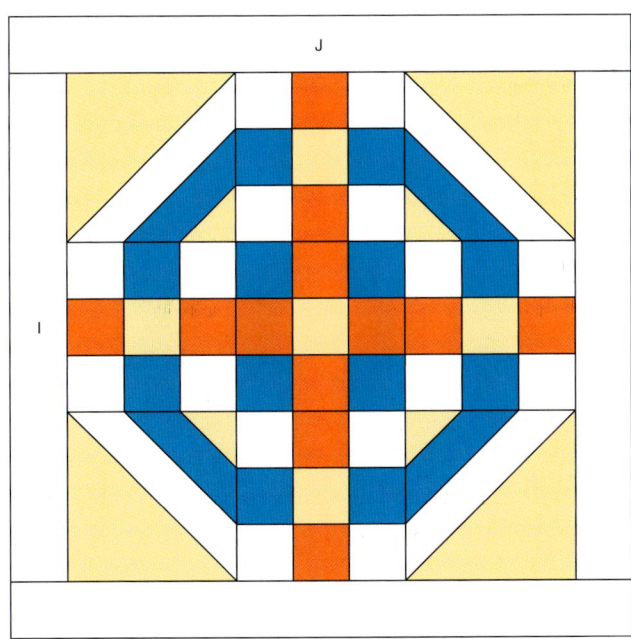

Nine-Patch Crossroads
Placement Diagram
22" x 22"

Linking Nine-Patches

Create a chain design using Nine-Patch and Roman Stripe blocks.

PROJECT SPECIFICATIONS
Skill Level: Beginner
Runner Size: 34" x 17"
Block Size: 6" x 6"
Number of Blocks: 10

MATERIALS
- 1 fat quarter each gold and olive green mottleds
- 1 fat quarter light blue print
- ⅓ yard green tonal
- ⅜ yard medium blue print
- Backing 40" x 23"
- Batting 40" x 23"
- All-purpose thread to match fabrics
- Quilting thread
- Basic sewing tools and supplies

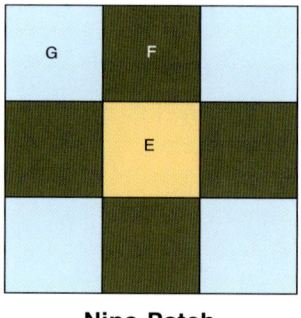

Nine-Patch
6" x 6" Block
Make 4

Roman Stripe
6" x 6" Block
Make 6

Cutting

1. Make six copies of the Roman Stripe Paper-Piecing Pattern on page 31.

2. Cut six 2" x 10" A strips and two 2½" x 21" G strips light blue print.

3. Cut one 3¼" x 21" strip light blue print; subcut strip into three 3¼" squares. Cut each square in half on one diagonal to make six C triangles.

4. Cut one 2½" x 21" E strip gold mottled.

5. Cut six 2" x 7" B strips and three 2½" x 21" F strips olive green mottled.

6. Cut one 9¾" x 9¾" square medium blue print; cut the square on both diagonals to make four H triangles.

7. Cut three 6⅞" x 6⅞" squares medium blue print; cut each square in half on one diagonal to make six D triangles.

8. Cut three 2¼" by fabric width strips green tonal for binding.

Completing the Roman Stripe Blocks

1. Complete four Roman Stripe triangle units using A and B strips and C triangles and referring to the General Instructions on page 29.

2. Add a D triangle to the A side of each unit to complete six Roman Stripe blocks referring to the block drawing.

Completing the Nine-Patch Blocks

1. Sew an E strip between two F strips with right sides together along the length to make an E-F strip set; press seams toward F strips.

2. Subcut the E-F strip set into four 2½" E-F units as shown in Figure 1.

Figure 1

3. Sew an F strip between two G strips with right sides together along the length to make an F-G strip set; press seams toward F.

Continued on page 25

Nine-Patches on Parade

Nine-Patch blocks and Half Log-Cabin blocks make this runner easy to piece in either a Western or bright orange color combination.

PROJECT SPECIFICATIONS
Skill Level: Beginner
Runner Size: 34" x 17"
Block Size: 6" x 6"
Number of Blocks: 10

MATERIALS
- 1 fat quarter each dark orange batik, medium orange batik, light orange print and gold mottled or
- 1 fat quarter each brown mottled (C), aqua tonal (A), rust tonal (E and F) and tan print (B and D)
- Backing 35" x 18"
- Batting 35" x 18"
- All-purpose thread to match fabrics
- Quilting thread
- 1 (1½") and 2 (1") silver conchos with leather ties (optional)
- Basic sewing tools and supplies

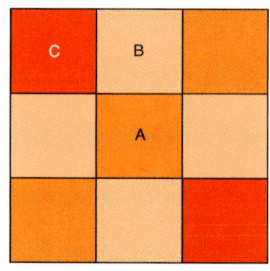

Orange Nine-Patch
6" x 6" Block
Make 4

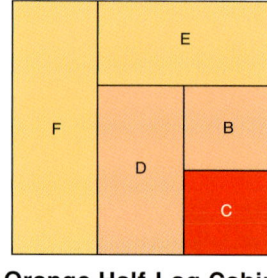

Orange Half-Log Cabin
6" x 6" Block
Make 6

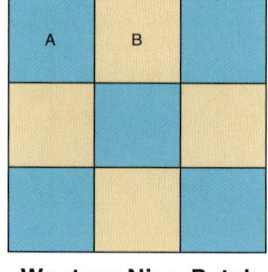

Western Nine-Patch
6" x 6" Block
Make 4

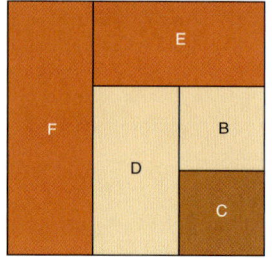

Western Half-Log Cabin
6" x 6" Block
Make 6

Cutting
Note: Cutting instructions are given for the orange version of the runner. Substitute fabrics for pieces as labeled on the block drawings for the alternate blocks.

1. Cut two 2½" x 21" A strips medium orange batik. **Note:** *For the Western runner, cut three 2½" x 21" A strips.*

2. Cut four 2½" x 21" B strips light orange print.

3. Cut one 4½" x 21" strip light orange print; subcut strip into six 2½" D pieces.

4. Cut two 2½" x 21" C strips dark orange batik. **Note:** *For Western runner, cut only one 2½" x 21" C strip.*

5. Cut one 4½" x 21" strip gold mottled; subcut strip into six 2½" E pieces.

6. Cut one 6½" x 21" strip gold mottled; subcut strip into six 2½" F pieces.

Completing the Nine-Patch Blocks

1. Sew an A strip between two B strips with right sides together along the length to make a B-A-B strip set; press seams toward A.

2. Subcut the B-A-B strip set into four 2½" B-A-B units as shown in Figure 1.

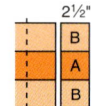

Figure 1

3. Sew an A strip to a B strip to a C strip with right sides together along the length to make an A-B-C strip set; press seams toward A and C.

4. Subcut the A-B-C strip set into eight 2½" A-B-C units as shown in Figure 2. *Note: For the Western runner, make an A-B-A strip set and subcut it into eight A-B-A units as shown in Figure 3.*

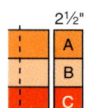 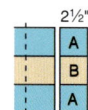

Figure 2   **Figure 3**

5. To complete one Nine-Patch block, sew a B-A-B unit between two A-B-C units as shown in Figure 4; press seams toward the B-A-B unit. Repeat to make four Orange Nine-Patch blocks. *Note: To complete one Western Nine-Patch block, use A-B-A units instead of the A-B-C units.*

Figure 4

Completing the Half-Log Cabin Blocks

1. Sew a B strip to a C strip with right sides together along the length; press seam toward C.

2. Subcut the strip set into six 2½" B-C units as shown in Figure 5.

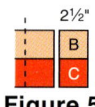

Figure 5   **Figure 6**

3. To complete one Half-Log Cabin block, sew D to a B-C unit as shown in Figure 6; press seam toward D.

4. Add E and then F to complete one block referring to the block drawing; press seams toward E and then F. Repeat to make six Orange Half-Log Cabin blocks.

Completing the Runner

1. Arrange and join the blocks in diagonal rows referring to Figure 7; press seams in adjacent rows in opposite directions.

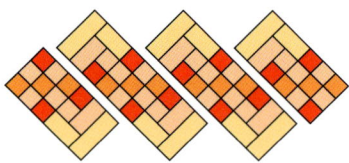

Figure 7

2. Join the rows to complete the pieced top referring to the Placement Diagram for positioning; press seams in one direction.

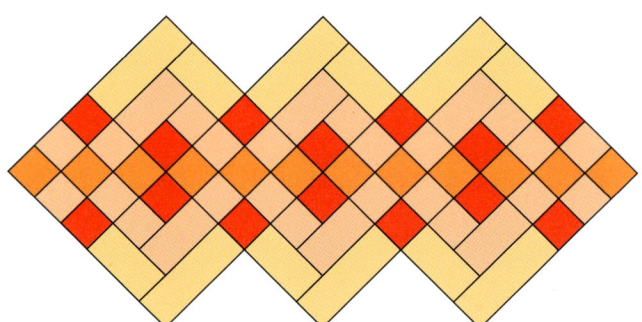

Nine-Patches On Parade
Placement Diagram
34" x 17"

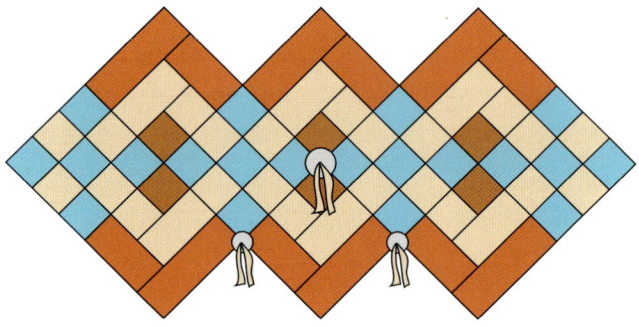

Western Nine-Patches On Parade
Placement Diagram
34" x 17"

Continued on page 28

Cactus Flowers in a Row

Twelve identical blocks join to make this pretty table runner.

PROJECT SPECIFICATIONS
Skill Level: Beginner
Runner Size: 42" x 18"
Block Size: 6" x 6"
Number of Blocks: 12

MATERIALS
- ⅛ yard red mottled
- ¼ yard green tonal
- ½ yard blue mottled
- ⅔ yard white tonal
- Backing 46" x 22"
- Batting 46" x 22"
- All-purpose thread to match fabrics
- Quilting thread
- Basic sewing tools and supplies

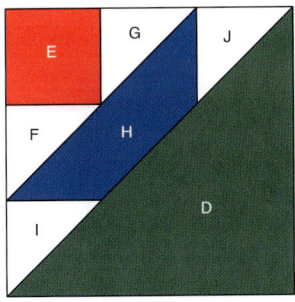

Cactus Flower
6" x 6" Block

Cutting

1. Make 12 copies of the Cactus Flower Paper-Piecing Pattern on page 31.

2. Cut four 2" by fabric width strips white tonal; subcut one strip into two 20" A strips. Join the remaining strips to make one long strip; press seams open. Subcut strip into two 44" C strips.

3. Cut two 3¼" by fabric width strips white tonal; subcut strips into (24) 3¼" squares. Cut each square in half on one diagonal to make 48 total triangles for F, G, I and J.

4. Cut four 2" by fabric width strips blue mottled. Subcut one strip into two 20" B strips. Join the remaining strips on the short ends to make one long strip; press seams open. Subcut strip into two 44" K strips.

5. Cut two 2" by fabric width strips blue mottled; subcut strips into (12) 7" H strips.

6. Cut one 3" by fabric width strip red mottled; subcut strip into (12) 3" E squares.

7. Cut one 6⅞" by fabric width strip green tonal; subcut strip into six 6⅞" squares. Cut each square in half on one diagonal to make 12 D triangles.

Completing the Blocks

1. Complete 12 Cactus Flower paper-pieced triangle units referring to the General Instructions and Figure 1.

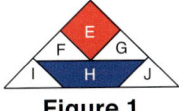

Figure 1

2. Sew a D triangle to a pieced unit to complete one Cactus Flower block referring to the block drawing; press seams toward D. Repeat to make 12 blocks.

Completing the Runner

1. Join two Cactus Flower blocks to make a row as shown in Figure 2; press seam in one direction. Repeat to make six rows; press seams in three rows in one direction and in the remaining three rows in the opposite direction.

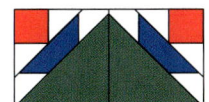

Figure 2

2. Join three rows to make half of the runner top, alternating seam allowance pressing; press seams in one direction. Repeat for the second half.

3. Join the two pieced halves to complete the runner top.

4. Sew an A strip to a B strip with right sides together along the length; press seams toward B.

5. Sew a C strip to a K strip with right sides together along the length; press seams toward K.

6. Center and sew an A-B strip to opposite short ends and the C-K strips to opposite long sides of the pieced center, mitering corners. Trim mitered seams to ¼"; press seams open to complete the pieced top.

7. Lay the batting on a flat surface; place the prepared backing piece right side up on top of the batting and the pieced top right sides together with the backing; pin layers to hold flat. Trim excess batting and backing even with the pieced top.

8. Sew all around edges, leaving a 6" opening on one end; trim batting close to stitching and clip corners.

9. Turn right side out through the opening. Press opening edges under ¼"; hand or machine-stitch opening closed.

10. Quilt as desired by hand or machine to finish. ∎

Above: Make the Cactus Flowers in a Row runner using earth-tone clors for your autumn table.

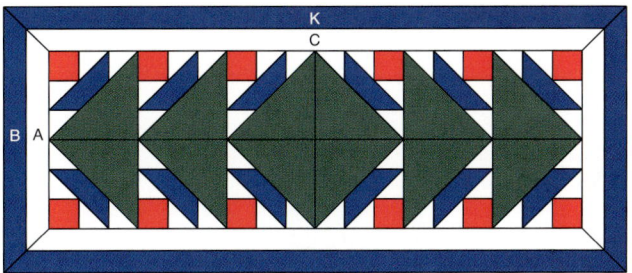

Cactus Flowers in a Row
Placement Diagram
42" x 18"

Cactus Flower Square

Roman Stripe blocks make the corners of this cheery Cactus Flower project.

PROJECT SPECIFICATIONS
Skill Level: Beginner
Quilt Size: 24" x 24"
Block Size: 6" x 6"
Number of Blocks: 16

MATERIALS
- ⅛ yard dark orange print
- ¼ yard pale orange print
- ⅓ yard light orange tonal
- ½ yard medium orange print
- ½ yard yellow print
- Backing 30" x 30"
- Batting 30" x 30"
- All-purpose thread to match fabrics
- Quilting thread
- Basic sewing tools and supplies

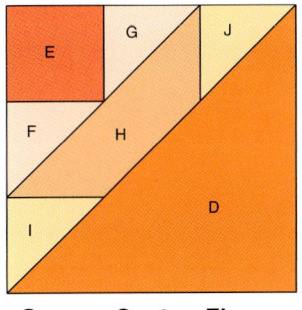

Orange Cactus Flower
6" x 6" Block
Make 4

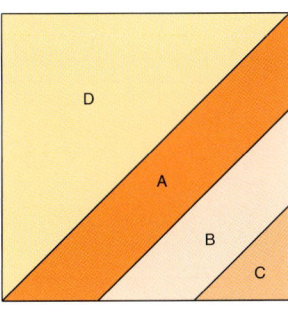

Roman Stripe
6" x 6" Block
Make 4

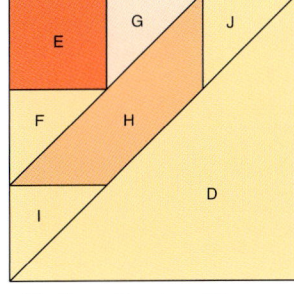

Yellow Cactus Flower
6" x 6" Block
Make 4

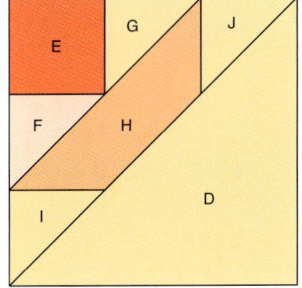

Reversed Yellow Cactus Flower
6" x 6" Block
Make 4

Cutting

1. Make 12 copies of the Cactus Flower Paper-Piecing Pattern on page 31.

2. Make four copies of the Roman Stripes Paper-Piecing Pattern on page 31.

3. Cut one 3¼" by fabric width strip pale orange print; subcut strip into eight 3¼" squares. Cut each square in half on one diagonal to make 16 total triangles for F and G.

4. Cut one 2" by fabric width strip pale orange print; subcut strip into four 7" B strips.

5. Cut two 2" by fabric width strips light orange tonal; subcut strips into (12) 7" H strips.

6. Cut two 3¼" x 3¼" squares light orange tonal; cut each square in half on one diagonal to make four C triangles.

7. Cut one 3" by fabric width strip dark orange print; subcut strip into (12) 3" E squares.

8. Cut one 6⅞" by fabric width strip medium orange print; subcut strip into two 6⅞" squares. Cut each square in half on one diagonal to make four D triangles.

9. Cut the remainder of the 6⅞"-wide strip from step 8 into four 2" x 10" A strips.

10. Cut three 2¼" by fabric width strips medium orange print for binding.

11. Cut one 6⅞" by fabric width strip yellow print; subcut strip into six 6⅞" squares. Cut each square in half on one diagonal to make 12 D triangles.

12. Cut two 3¼" by fabric width strips yellow print; subcut strips into (16) 3¼" squares. Cut each square in half on one diagonal to make 32 triangles total for F, G, I and J.

Completing the Cactus Flower Blocks

1. Complete 12 Cactus Flower paper-pieced triangle units referring to the General Instructions and Figure 1 for color placement.

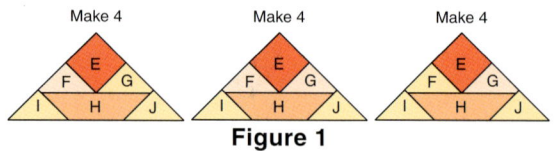

Figure 1

2. Sew a medium orange D triangle to four pieced units to complete one Orange Cactus Flower block referring to the block drawing; press seams toward D.

3. Sew a yellow print D triangle to each of the remaining pieced units to complete four each Yellow Cactus Flower and Reversed Yellow Cactus Flower blocks referring to the block drawings; press seams toward D.

Completing the Roman Stripe Blocks

1. Complete four Roman Stripe paper-pieced triangle units using A and B strips and C triangles and referring to the General Instructions on page 29.

2. Add a yellow print D triangle to the A side of each unit to complete four Roman Stripe blocks referring to the block drawing.

Completing the Quilt

1. Join two Roman Stripe blocks with one each Yellow and Reversed Yellow Cactus Flower Blocks to make a row as shown in Figure 2; press seams in one direction. Repeat to make two rows.

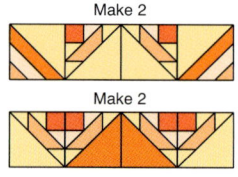

Figure 2

2. Join two Orange Cactus Flower Blocks with one each Yellow and Reversed Yellow Cactus Flower block to make a row, again referring to Figure 2; press seams in one direction. Repeat to make two rows.

3. Join the rows to complete the pieced top; press seams in one direction.

4. Complete the quilt using the prepared backing and batting pieces and the cut binding strips referring to Completing Your Quilt on page 30. ■

Cactus Flower Square
Placement Diagram
24" x 24"

Cactus Flower Octagon

Arrange the two different-color Cactus Flower blocks with plain triangles and the result is an octagon-shaped topper.

PROJECT SPECIFICATIONS
Skill Level: Beginner
Quilt Size: 24" x 24"
Block Size: 6" x 6"
Number of Blocks: 12

MATERIALS
- ⅛ yard orange print
- ¼ yard each white and blue tonals
- ¼ yard green mottled
- ⅜ yard gold mottled
- ½ yard orange mottled
- Backing 30" x 30"
- Batting 30" x 30"
- All-purpose thread to match fabrics
- Quilting thread
- Basic sewing tools and supplies

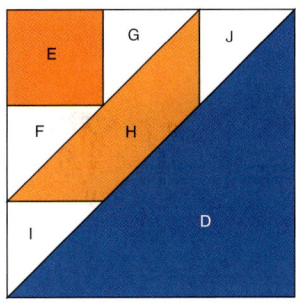

Blue Cactus Flower
6" x 6" Block
Make 8

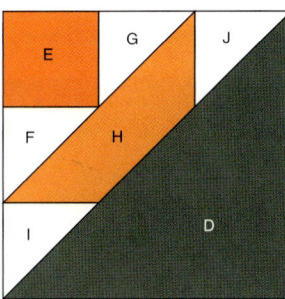

Green Cactus Flower
6" x 6" Block
Make 4

Cutting
1. Make 12 copies of the Cactus Flower Paper-Piecing Pattern on page 31.

2. Cut one 9¾" x 9¾" square gold mottled; cut the square on both diagonals to make four A triangles.

3. Cut two 6⅞" x 6⅞" squares green mottled; cut each square in half on one diagonal to make four green D triangles.

4. Cut four 6⅞" x 6⅞" squares blue tonal; cut each square in half on one diagonal to make eight blue D triangles.

5. Cut one 3" by fabric width strip orange print; subcut strip into (12) 3" E squares.

6. Cut two 3¼" by fabric width strips white tonal; subcut strips into (24) 3¼" squares. Cut each square in half on one diagonal to make 48 total triangles for F, G, I and J.

7. Cut two 2" by fabric width strips orange mottled; subcut strips into (12) 7" H strips.

8. Cut three 2¼" by fabric width strips orange mottled for binding.

Completing the Blocks
1. Complete 12 Cactus Flower paper-pieced triangle units referring to the General Instructions and Figure 1.

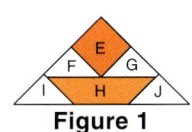

Figure 1

2. Sew a blue D triangle to eight pieced units to complete eight Blue Cactus Flower blocks and a

green D triangle to four pieced units to complete four Green Cactus Flower blocks referring to the block drawings; press seams toward D.

Completing the Quilt

1. Join two Blue Cactus Flower blocks with two A triangles to make the top row as shown in Figure 2; press seams in one direction. Repeat to make the bottom row.

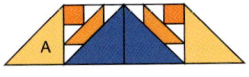
Figure 2

Figure 3

2. Join two Blue Cactus Flower blocks with two Green Cactus Flower blocks to make a center row as shown in Figure 3; press seams in one direction. Repeat to make two center rows.

3. Join the two center rows and add the top and bottom rows referring to the Placement Diagram for positioning; press seams in one direction.

4. Complete the quilt using the prepared backing and batting pieces and the cut binding strips referring to Completing Your Quilt on page 30.

Cactus Flower Octagon
Placement Diagram
24" x 24"

Linking Nine-Patches
Continued from page 13

4. Subcut the F-G strip set into eight 2½" F-G units as shown in Figure 2.

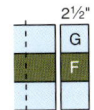
Figure 2   **Figure 3**

5. Sew an E-F unit between two F-G units to complete one Nine-Patch block referring to Figure 3; press seams away from the center unit. Repeat to make four Nine-Patch blocks.

Completing the Runner

1. Arrange and join the pieced blocks with the H triangles in diagonal rows as shown in Figure 4; press seams in adjacent rows in opposite directions.

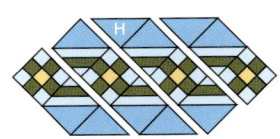
Figure 4

2. Join the rows to complete the pieced top; press seams in one direction.

3. Complete the runner using the prepared backing and batting pieces and the cut binding strips referring to Completing Your Quilt on page 30.

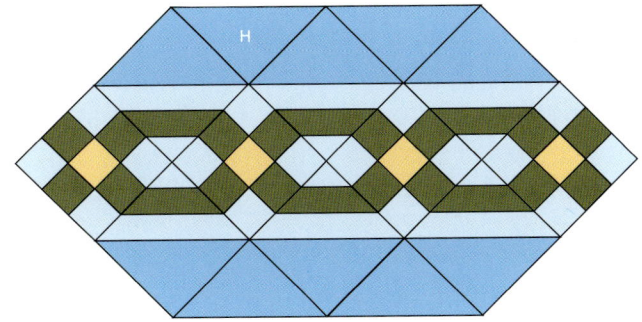
Linking Nine-Patches
Placement Diagram
34" x 17"

Cactus Flower Hexagon Place Mats

Make a set of four place mats using Cactus Flower blocks.

PROJECT SPECIFICATIONS
Skill Level: Beginner
Place Mat Size: 22¾" x 12½"
Block Size: 6" x 6"
Number of Blocks: 8
Number of Place Mats: 4

MATERIALS
- ⅛ yard yellow tonal
- ¼ yard dark green batik
- ¼ yard blue tonal
- ⅜ yard white tonal
- ⅔ yard light olive tonal
- 1¼ yards backing fabric
- 4 (25" x 14") rectangles batting
- All-purpose thread to match fabrics
- Quilting thread
- Basic sewing tools and supplies

Cutting

1. Make eight copies of the Cactus Flower Paper-Piecing Pattern on page 31.

2. Cut one 9¾" by fabric width strip white tonal; subcut strip into two 9¾" squares. Cut each square on both diagonals to make eight K triangles.

3. Cut the remainder of the strip cut in step 2 into three 3¼"-wide strips; subcut strips into (16) 3¼" squares. Cut each square in half on one diagonal to make 32 total F, G, I and J triangles.

4. Cut one 6⅞" by fabric width strip blue tonal; subcut strip into four 6⅞" squares. Cut each square in half on one diagonal to make eight D triangles.

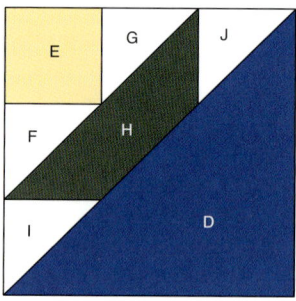

Cactus Flower
6" x 6" Block

5. Cut one 3" by fabric width strip yellow tonal; subcut strip into eight 3" E squares.

6. Cut two 2" by fabric width strips dark green batik; subcut strips into eight 7" H strips.

7. Cut eight 2½" by fabric width strips light green tonal; subcut strips into eight each 7" A, 9" B and 16" C strips.

8. Cut four 25" x 14" rectangles backing fabric as shown in Figure 1.

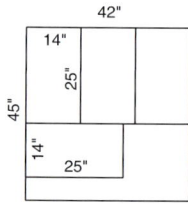

Figure 1

Figure 2

Completing the Blocks

1. Complete eight Cactus Flower paper-pieced triangle units referring to the General Instructions and Figure 2.

2. Sew a D triangle to each pieced unit to complete eight Cactus Flower blocks referring to the block drawing; press seams toward D.

Completing the Place Mats

1. To complete one place mat, arrange two K triangles with two pieced blocks as shown in Figure 3; join to make two rows. Press seams toward K. Join the rows to complete the pieced center.

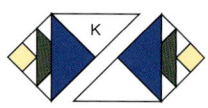

Figure 3

2. Sew an A strip to opposite ends of the pieced center and trim the A end even as shown in Figure 4; press seams toward A strips.

3. Add the B strips and trim as in step 2, again referring to Figure 4; press seams toward B. Repeat with with C strips on opposite long sides to complete one place mat top; press seams toward C strips. Repeat to make four place mat tops.

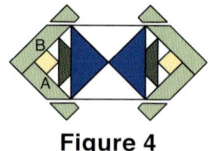

Figure 4

4. Lay the batting on a flat surface; place the prepared backing piece right side up on top of the batting and the pieced top right sides together with the backing; pin layers to hold flat. Trim excess batting and backing even with the pieced top.

5. Sew all around edges, leaving a 6" opening on one end; trim batting close to stitching and clip corners.

6. Turn right side out through the opening. Press opening edges under ¼"; hand- or machine-stitch opening closed.

7. Quilt as desired by hand or machine to finish.

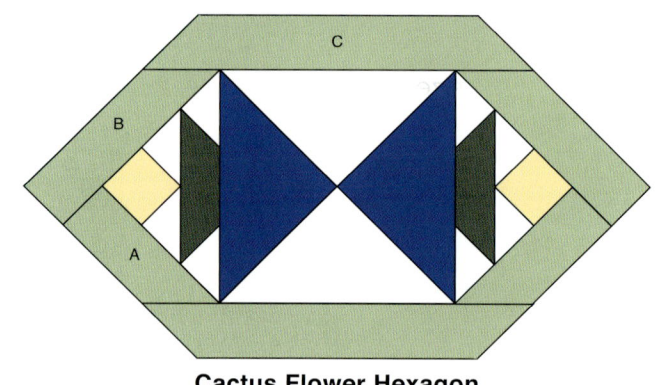

Cactus Flower Hexagon
Placement Diagram
22¾" x 12½"

Nine-Patches on Parade

Continued from page 16

3. Lay the batting on a flat surface; place the prepared backing piece right side up on top of the batting and the pieced top right sides together with the backing; pin layers to hold flat. Trim excess batting and backing even with the pieced top.

4. Sew all around edges, leaving a 6" opening on one end; trim batting close to stitching and clip corners.

5. Turn right side out through the opening. Press opening edges under ¼"; hand- or machine-stitch opening closed.

6. Quilt as desired by hand or machine to finish. *Note: Sew conchos with leather ties to the Western version of the runner referring to project photo for positioning.*

General Instructions

The pieced triangle units in the Roman Stripes and Cactus Rose blocks are paper-pieced. The patterns given on page 31 are copied as directed with individual patterns. The cutting instructions given with each project list the fabrics needed to complete the paper-pieced units. Refer to the following paper-piecing instructions to complete the units. Finish your quilt referring to Completing Your Quilt.

Preparing Patterns

• Paper-piecing patterns may be photocopied for stitching. Check that the photocopied image is the same size as the original. Many photocopiers distort the image. A change in size, however slight, may make a difference in the overall piecing of your block. Also, check the photocopied pattern to be sure the ink will not come off on your iron when pressing pieces while sewing.

• To make the patterns by hand, use a permanent pen or pencil to exactly trace the patterns. Beware of any ink that may run. In heavily stitched areas, the paper foundation may not be entirely removed. Future washing may cause any ink left within the stitching to run.

Stitching Patterns

• Begin with a sharp needle in your sewing machine. Shorten your stitch length to 18–20 stitches per inch. This shorter stitch length allows for easy removal of the paper without stretching the stitches.

• Use thread to match fabrics or a neutral color that will blend with all the fabrics.

• Place fabric to cover area A on the paper pattern with wrong side of fabric against the unmarked side of the paper, allowing fabric to extend at least ¼" into adjacent areas as shown in Figure 1.

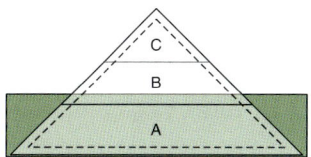

Figure 1

• Place fabric for area B right sides together with fabric A on the A-B edge as shown in Figure 2; pin along the A-B line. Fold fabric B over to cover area B, allowing fabric to extend at least ¼" into adjacent areas as shown in Figure 3. Adjust fabric if necessary. Unfold fabric B to lie flat on fabric A.

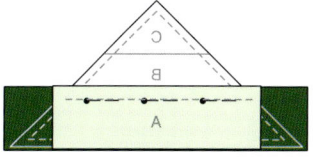

Figure 2

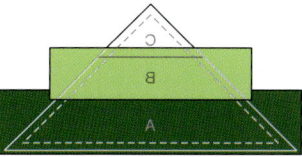

Figure 3

• Flip paper pattern; stitch on the A-B line, stitching to or beyond the outside heavy solid line on outer edges as shown in Figure 4. ***Note:** Begin and end 2 or 3 stitches into adjacent areas on inside seam intersections as shown in Figure 5.*

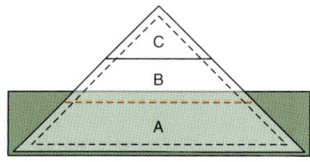

Figure 4

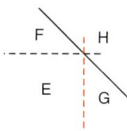

Figure 5

- Trim the A-B seam allowance to ⅛"–¼" as shown in Figure 6. Fold fabric B to cover area B; lightly press with a warm dry iron.

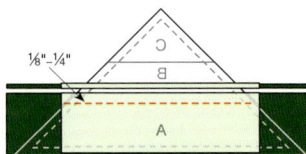

Figure 6

- Continue to add fabrics in alphabetical order to cover the paper pattern as shown in Figure 7. Check that each piece will cover its area before stitching. The very short stitches are hard to remove and often cause a tear in the paper pattern. Should this happen, place a small piece of transparent tape over the tear to continue to use the pattern. Do not use this quick fix frequently, as it makes removal of the paper difficult.

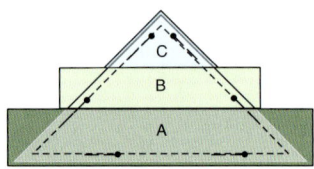

Figure 7

- Pin outside fabric edges to the paper pattern. Trim paper and fabric edges even on the outside heavy solid line as shown in Figure 8.

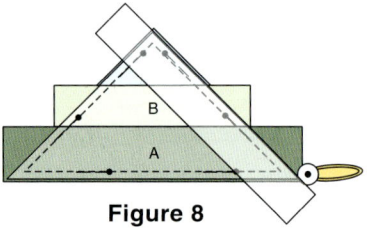

Figure 8

- Leave paper pattern intact until the block is joined with other quilt pieces, then remove all paper.

Completing Your Quilt

1. Mark quilting lines onto the finished top as desired. **Note:** *The sample projects were all machine-quilted by stitching in the ditch of seams with coordinating thread. Three included machine stippling in large unpieced areas. Those without binding were machine-stitched ¼" from outside edges all around.*

2. Sandwich the batting between the completed top and prepared backing; pin or baste layers together to hold. **Note:** *If using basting spray to hold layers together, refer to instructions on the product container for use.*

3. Quilt as desired by hand or machine; remove pins or basting. Trim excess backing and batting even with quilt top.

4. Join binding strips on short ends to make one long strip; press seams open. Fold the strip in half along length with wrong sides together; press.

5. Sew binding to quilt edges, mitering corners and overlapping ends. Fold binding to the back side and stitch in place to finish. ■

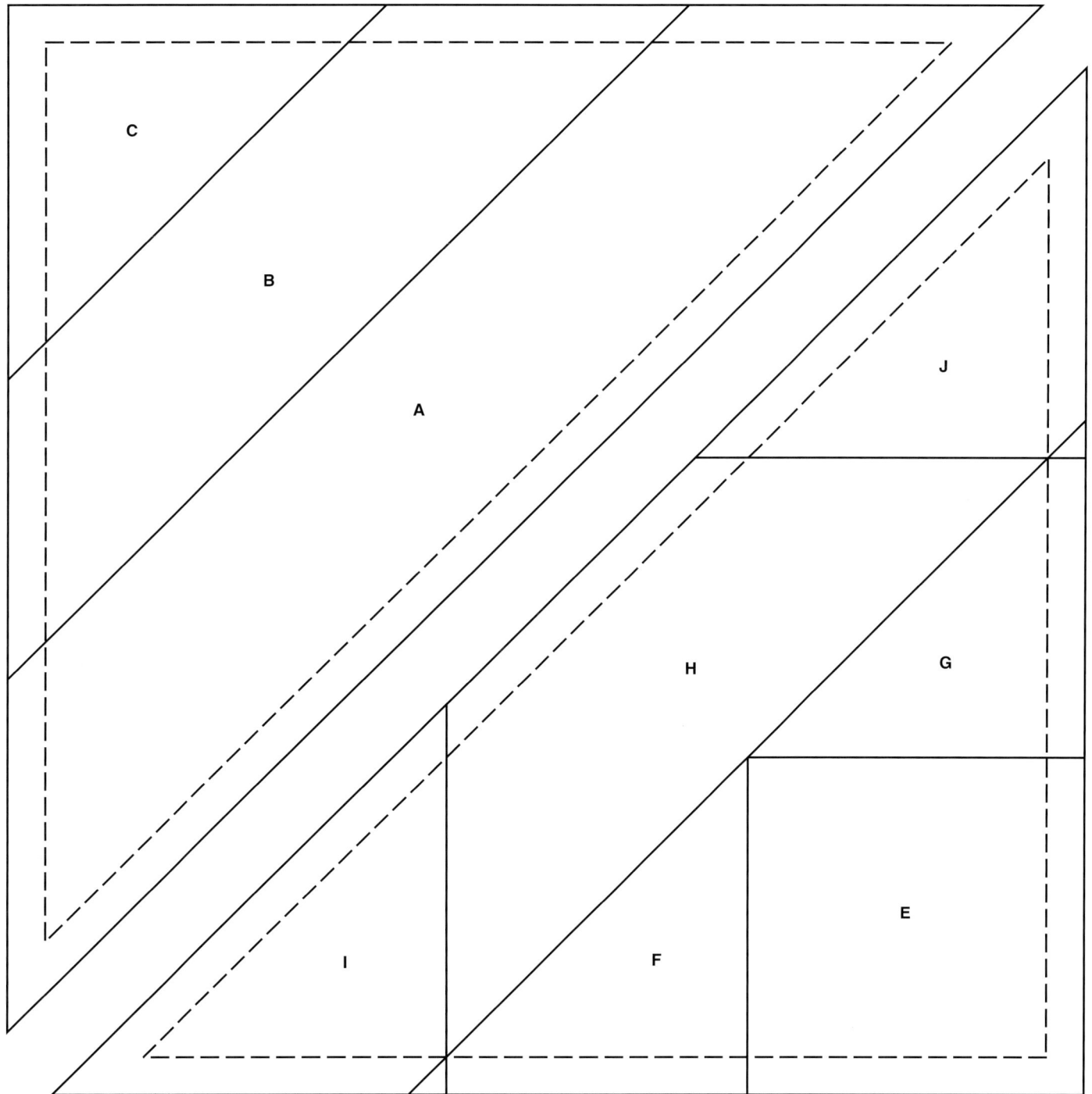

Roman Stripe Paper-Piecing Pattern
Make copies as indicated in project instructions.

Cactus Flower Paper-Piecing Pattern
Make copies as indicated in project instructions.

Roman Stripe Festival

Continued from page 8

2. Sew E to F; press seam toward F.

3. Add G, H and I in alphabetical order to complete one Blue Log Cabin block referring to Figure 2; press seams toward last rectangle added.

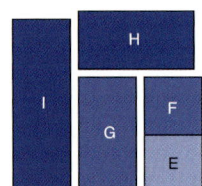

Figure 2

4. Repeat steps 2 and 3 to make four each Blue and Red Log Cabin blocks.

Completing the Quilt

1. Arrange and join blocks in rows referring to Figure 3, making two of each row; press seams in adjacent rows in opposite directions.

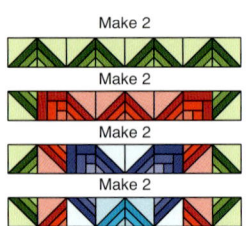

Figure 3

2. Arrange and join the rows to complete the pieced top referring to the Placement Diagram for positioning of rows; press seams in one direction.

3. Complete the quilt using the prepared backing and batting pieces and the cut binding strips referring to Completing Your Quilt on page 30. ■

Roman Stripe Festival
Placement Diagram
48" x 48"

Nine-Patch/Roman Stripe Topper (page 2), Linking Nine-Patches (page 12) and Cactus Flower Square (page 21) machine-quilted by Jeri Middleton.

Nine-Patches on Parade (page 14) stitched and machine-quilted by Nancy K. Britton.

E-mail: Customer_Service@whitebirches.com

Simple Shapes Table Toppers is published by DRG, 306 East Parr Road, Berne, IN 46711, telephone (260) 589-4000. Printed in USA. Copyright © 2007 DRG. All rights reserved. This publication may not be reproduced in part or in whole without written permission from the publisher.

RETAIL STORES: If you would like to carry this pattern book or any other House of White Birches publications, call the Wholesale Department at Annie's Attic to set up a direct account: (903) 636-4303. Also, request a complete listing of publications available from House of White Birches.

Every effort has been made to ensure that the instructions in this pattern book are complete and accurate. We cannot, however, take responsibility for human error, typographical mistakes or variations in individual work.

ISBN: 978-1-59217-177-4
1 2 3 4 5 6 7 8 9

Editors: Jeanne Stauffer, Sandra L. Hatch
Associate Editor: Dianne Schmidt
Technical Artist: Connie Rand
Copy Supervisor: Michelle Beck
Copy Editors: Sue Harvey, Nicki Lehman, Mary O'Donnell, Judy Weatherford
Graphic Arts Supervisor: Ronda Bechinski

Graphic Artist: Nicole Gage
Art Director: Brad Snow
Assistant Art Director: Nick Pierce
Photography: Tammy Christian, Don Clark, Matthew Owen, Jackie Schaffel
Photo Stylists: Tammy Nussbaum, Tammy M. Smith